This Book Belongs to

_____

Lover of Flea Markets

Before & After — now there's a phrase! If you "flea market," you know the "before" can refer to the boring time **before** discovering the endless joys of tag sales, secondhand shops, and weekend junking. And **after**? Once you've discovered the fun, you can't help but visit your favorite stores on a regular basis. And when the hunt is over and the bargains are made, finding a place to display those newfound treasures is the most enjoyable part of it all. Hauling new favorite objects out of the car and into your home to be carefully enshrined in their rightful place of honor has an indescribable **afterglow** that only a true treasure hound knows.

However, there are those occasional treasures that need more than soap and water to truly shine. This book is filled with such items and lots of ideas for **Before & After** makeovers. As you will see in the photos, some of our transformations are pretty dramatic! We've included instant ideas and other projects that may involve adding a little paint or fabric, but all can be accomplished in less than a weekend — many in less than an hour!

During my shopping adventures (can you believe I get paid to do this?), I searched for items large and small, both commonplace and unusual. This book proves that thrift shop bargains, from baking sheets to piano parts, can become inspired additions to any decorating scheme. In your travels, always be on the lookout for items that have possibilities for new life and function. Then, let the **Before & After** fun begin! Who knew that an oversized bedroom dresser could make such a beautiful dining room server? Or that outdated coffee tables could come back in their next life as stylish ottomans?

When you set out on your next hunting expedition, keep your mind open to the unexpected. It is the things you passionately hunt, buy, and collect that tell your stories and define your own personal style. And remember, **before** you begin your own projects, take the photos that will prove your creative genius — **after**!

Enjoy the search,

Patti Uhiren

Patti Uhiren

FLEA MARKET FINDS
Before & After
HOME DECORATING WITH MAKEOVER MIRACLES

EDITORIAL STAFF

Vice President and Editor-in-Chief: Sandra Graham Case. *Executive Director of Publications:* Cheryl Nodine Gunnells. *Special Projects Design Director:* Patricia Wallenfang Uhiren. *Senior Publications Designer:* Dana Vaughn. *Senior Publications Director:* Susan White Sullivan. *Book Publications Director:* Kristine Anderson Mertes. *Editorial Director:* Susan Frantz Wiles. *Photography Director:* Karen Hall. *Art Operations Director:* Jeff Curtis. TECHNICAL — *Technical Editor:* Leslie Schick Gorrell. *Book Coordinator and Senior Technical Writer:* Shawnna B. Manes. *Technical Associate:* Theresa Hicks Young. *Design Assistant:* Karla Edgar. EDITORIAL — *Managing Editor:* Alan Caudle. *Senior Associate Editor:* Susan McManus Johnson. ART — *Art Publications Director:* Rhonda Shelby. *Art Imaging Director:* Mark Hawkins. *Imaging Technician:* Mark Potter. *Art Category Manager:* Lora Puls. *Staff Photographer:* Russell Ganser. *Publishing Systems Administrator:* Becky Riddle. *Publishing Systems Assistants:* Clint Hanson, Myra S. Means, John Rose, and Chris Wertenberger.

BUSINESS STAFF

Publisher: Rick Barton. *Vice President, Finance:* Tom Siebenmorgen. *Director of Corporate Planning and Development:* Laticia Dittrich. *Vice President, Retail Marketing:* Bob Humphrey. *Vice President, Sales:* Ray Shelgosh. *Vice President, National Accounts:* Pam Stebbins. *Director of Sales and Services:* Margaret Reinold. *Vice President, Operations:* Jim Dittrich. *Comptroller, Operations:* Rob Thieme. *Retail Customer Service Manager:* Stan Raynor. *Print Production Manager:* Fred F. Pruss.

Made in the United States of America

Library of Congress Control Number 2003112561
Hardcover ISBN 1-57486-296-0
Softcover ISBN 1-57486-297-9

10 9 8 7 6 5 4 3 2 1

10

30

32

40

42

Contents

16

20

24

28

34

36

38

44

47

48

50

52

54

66

68

70

84

86

88

Contents

CONTINUED

56

62

64

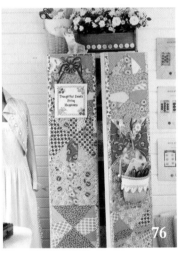

76

80

82

90

92

94

96

98

100

110

114

116

128

130

132

 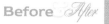

Contents
CONTINUED

104

106

108

118

122

126

134

Before&After

Fifties Flair

Flea market furnishings can be design classics just as they are. Then again, a new touch of color or an updated fabric can bridge the decades to put original flair on retro style. In the next few pages, these old pieces from the 1950's move forward in time. Follow along to see the "swell" switcheroos that anyone can do — but only if they know your secrets!

Before & After

Razzle-Dazzle! A lamp from the Rocket Age goes off — and on — with brilliant results. See page 150 for the formula to cover your lampshade with the fabric and trim of your choice. The lamp needs only a touch of easy-to-apply silver leaf on its base, socket casing, and finial.

You could almost read by the glow of this magazine rack, but it's really just reflections off the new gold spray paint and silver leaf. Once you paint your magazine caddy, mask off the wire frame, place newspaper inside the holder, then apply spray adhesive and silver leaf to the pierced metal.

Before&After

We may call it "silver" or "platinum" today, but in Fifties lingo the hip phrase was "chrome-plated." Actually, the inset in this tabletop (page 135) is stainless steel tile, and it comes pre-assembled on a grid, so you don't have to place each tile individually. The retro chair has a new seat covering of gigantic polka-dots. And it's a redo that's a breeze to complete — just spray paint the chair brown, apply silver leaf to the chairback, and see page 135 to cover the seat.

A Change of Wardrobe

Tailor a shabby wardrobe into a suitable accessory for your continental décor. When your new cabinet is complete, you'll be ready to store helpful items, keep track of time, and jot down the day's menu of events — all in one place. Turn to page 135 to work this Before & After miracle with ease!

A Time and A Place for Everything

It would take a second glance for anyone to realize that this elegant clock doesn't have an enameled face, and yet it's a timepiece you can install in the cabinet of your choice just by following the quick instructions on page 135.

They're carefree, fun to use, and nearly indestructible ... wire baskets from the flea market can hold anything from eggs to flowers, and even the ingredients for salad! If the baskets you locate have a few spots of rust, just sand them away and apply a spray paint that's meant for metal.

Another multi-purpose item you don't want to overlook is the insulated drink container. When it isn't serving a temperature-perfect beverage, it's also a cheerful vase!

It's all in the details, and you'll love how simple it is to embellish your wooden cabinet with precut swirls and curves (page 135).

A
Toast to

Timelessness

Freshly hauled from the flea market and missing its doors, this old buffet has definitely seen better days — and yet, its future is bright! With a little Before & After magic, this castoff cabinet will give many more years of service with distinction.

Silver service to "de-light":

A graceful coffee urn reflects elegant style when topped with a lamp kit. To take your coffee urn from plain to perky, turn to page 136. And when browsing the flea market, be on the lookout for other unusual objects that can become creative lamps.

Fabric-covered foam core fills in the sides of our new bar. Of course, you'll want to start with the easy basics and paint your cabinet according to the simple directions on page 136. When your cabinet is ready, just slide a pair of wicker carry-alls into the storage space. This buffet/bar has a pleasant bonus to help you entertain … it rests on old-fashioned casters and can be moved from the kitchen to your favorite living space.

Something to Write Home About

One of the best things about flea market before-and-afters is that any secondhand item can be changed to fit your taste. But every now and then you'll find a real treasure, a classic item that only needs a little T.L.C. to make it fit your décor. This forgotten desk became the basis for a distinctive office, and with a minimum of fuss! See page 137 for the easy instructions.

A large amber glass bottle with its original label becomes a lamp with lots of character. To make this instant switch, we used a bottle adapter lamp kit (shown on page 136) and topped it with a woven lampshade — absolutely no wiring needed!

Getting down to brass tacks: Cork paper adds stylish texture to the top of this desk, while a glass top protects it from spills. Be sure and check your local flea markets for unusual collectibles, such as our shoeshine box, to organize your workspace. Flea markets offer thousands of items with a bonus quality you won't find anywhere else … a patina of age and memories.

Open the door to decorating possibilities with a unique memo board — it's as easy as turning to page 137. And don't close your mind to the fashionable appeal of old boxes. On pages 62 through 67, we show you how fabric, papers, and other ordinary materials can add excitement to all kinds of vintage containers.

To decorate a room with Eastern accents, you could visit every market from Hong Kong to the Polynesian islands. Or you could just take a little trip to your local flea market. At the heart of this exotic collection is the bamboo-trimmed dresser that's been restored with a few flicks of a paintbrush. This cultural exchange takes place on page 137.

EASTERN

INFLUENCE

TURNING THE TABLES...
INTO A
BENCH

When you decide to decorate, take advantage of the sturdiness of old-fashioned furniture. It's easy to do, and you'll be rewarded with years of reliable service. For instant seating that's also portable, just paint two wooden "step" tables in the colors of your choice, then "gift-wrap" a piece of foam rubber in an old blanket — we used a scrappy quilt top from the flea market. On page 32, we show how these same tables can brighten your outdoor living. And to coordinate your lamp with your bench, plug in to page 150 for instructions to cover the lampshade.

Before & After

In Living Color

The same sturdy "step" tables that worked together as a bench on page 30 are put to work as outdoor end tables on this colorful porch. We even used some of the same accessories — the overnight case now holds potted plants, and did you notice how different the lamp base looks with a crazy new shade? See page 150 to fashion your own wacky shade. To freshen an old sofa cushion, use large safety pins to secure a new fabric cover. Sprinkle the outdoor room with bright pillows and flea market collectibles (we're especially fond of our clown cookie jar "planter"), and you're ready for a season of fun.

Your friends will want to know where you found this daisy-fresh patio set. You could tell them that the chairs and part of the table came from the flea market. Or you could just say, "They're originals that can't be found in stores," because either response would be perfectly true. To decorate your outdoors with flower-child flair, turn to page 139. Groovy!

Please Don't Eat the Daisies

Impressive Exhibit

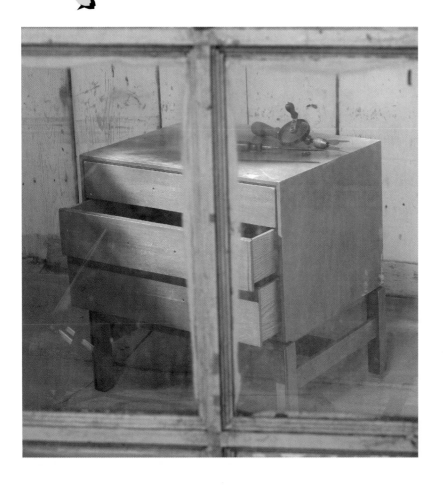

There's really no excuse for having plain, boxy furniture — not when it can exhibit this kind of artistic flair! Put your end table on display with poster-decked drawer fronts, sleek knobs, and matching paint. No fancy brushwork is needed to add this beauty to your collection; just turn to page 151 and select "Parsons Table" from our gallery of instructions.

For Your
Summer
Reading List

It's not always necessary to completely refinish a furniture find. Often new paint and a little sanding can give it a distressed look that suits your décor.

A bookseller's table was perfect for this technique. Found rough and worn, we left the original paint colors on the table and lightly sanded it to smooth any rough places. After wiping the table with a tack cloth, a coordinating paint color was added in several areas. The look was complete after randomly sanding the table again to reveal the wood and all the underlying paint colors.

A Bench Marked in History

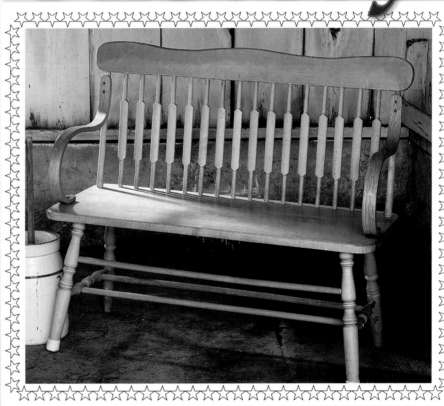

The glorious days of summer may be firecracker-hot, but a few lucky folks will remain cool and comfy on this patriotic porch. And there's no doubt that the focal point of this festive setting is the all-American bench. This fast Before & After gives an enthusiastic nod to our favorite flag, and it was done just by using red and blue paint and gluing seven wooden stars to the back. We folded a matching quilt for our seat cushion and added a couple of pillows to round out this heartfelt salute to an important holiday.

Over Easy & Farm Fresh

You don't have to rise with the chickens to finish this farm-fresh canister before breakfast. Wallpaper border goes on quick, adding rural charm to the lidded can. If your canister clashes with the border of your choice, just apply a coat of paint before the wallpaper — you'll still have a handy catch-all before the rooster stops crowing.

Fresh

"Who would ever buy that?" Damaged flea market items often inspire that question. With no top, this old table looks useless and unlovable even though its wooden structure is as sound as ever. When we realized a nearby enameled tabletop would be a perfect fit, we knew it was time for a quick makeover. New paint (page 140) made all the difference for both pieces, turning this tired utility table into a kitchen classic that's the center of attention in its new home. **"I'll take it!"**

Kitchen *for the*

Chances are, you'll find lots of old tumblers and glass caddies at your local flea market, so why not pick up a set for cabinet-to-table ease? After all, convenience is always in good taste.

Caddies
of a Different Sort

One twentieth-century invention that should never be discarded is the ever-useful tumbler caddy. These great little helpers can hold far more than just frosty beverage glasses. Use them to carry a selection of small things from place to place, or just fill them with a collection of nosegays and naturals — a quick and portable decorative accent!

A New Recipe

for Notes

DAIRY MADE ICE CREAM

"You're sure ~ It's pure"

Fred:
Feed chickens
Milk Cow
Paint Barn

Take note of these fast flea market fix-ups! A large baking sheet (opposite) tops the list with a coat of chalkboard paint and a tin sign. For magnetic memo minders that are right on the button (left and below), search old magazines and sewing baskets for fasteners or pictures to glue to craft magnets. They're sure to stick to an old pan lid or cookie sheet. Drill holes in the corners of your converted memo board, then use cord or ribbon for hangers.

Can you see the possibilities? A fabric-covered cardboard circle brightens the lid of our oversized peanut tin (below), while tempered glass tops it to create an instant table. Crackled paint and a wallpaper border set the scene on our fruit can (opposite). The top of the newly bountiful fruit table is a flea market find that may surprise you — it's an antique whisky barrel lid!

If You Think You Can –
You Can!

If you're spending too much time digging through papers on your kitchen table or desk, look for a flea market desk organizer with plenty of slots and drawers! This old-fashioned office assistant will help smooth out your paperwork.

EVERYTHING

Does kitchen clutter give you a sinking feeling? Tuck away unsightly necessities inside two sets of drawers from a sewing machine cabinet. Use spray adhesive to cover a board with fabric, place it atop the drawers, and you've got an instant shelf for displaying kitchen collectibles.

Dressed
for Dinner

Before we revamped it, this plain dresser was about as desirable as last year's fruitcake. Now, with its lovely stenciled roses, fresh door insets, and brushed pewter knobs, it's a gourmet confection for the dining room. To make your old dresser go from lackluster to luscious, see page 140.

When the decorating style you want seems to be eluding you, the flea market may very well have the answer. We find it's often a matter of watching for the right furniture style, rather than color or texture. The fact is, today's paints, fabrics, and wallpapers can do amazing things to the surfaces of home furnishings. This tasteful dining room is a case in point: Not one of the larger pieces remains in its original condition. The table, chairs, and large buffet are all Before & Afters. We share more details on the following pages …

Fine Dining Room

An entertainment center goes from the living room to the dining room. We removed the upper half, or shelving frame, leaving the cabinet part of the unit intact. Since the drawer pulls were only ornamental, we removed them from the cabinet as well, and filled in the holes with wood putty (see page 156 for instructions on preparing furniture for paint). Paint and three wooden cutouts gave the new buffet an equally new style.

And we didn't spend megabucks for a marble top, either. The secret? Faux marble wallpaper — who knew? We used a brayer to smooth the paper onto the buffet top, clipped the wallpaper at the corners, then used craft glue to secure the edges.

A rotary cutter and rotary ruler make this faux-finished tabletop come together in no time...our "marble" tiles are really cut from wallpaper! Start by cutting 4" and 1¹/₄" square tiles from coordinating pre-pasted wallpapers. Align the 4" tiles along the 45-degree and 1¹/₄" marks on the ruler and trim the corners. After adhering the tiles to the tabletop and trimming along the edges of the table, apply a sealer, then cover the tabletop with a piece of polished-edge glass.

Our dining set was formerly dulled by years of use, but now the light gleams wherever it touches the same ornate curves. The difference? An application of glossy paint now accentuates the graceful carving.

Don't think outside the box —
change it! This unusual tote was
created to carry wine bottles in its
cylindrical compartments. With a
basecoat of paint and a covering
of textured wallpaper, it has a
fresh new look as a bath caddy.

Little boxes only
need a padded lid
(use fabric, batting,
cardboard, and glue)
or a decoupaged
postcard to make
them unique. And a
box purse converts to
a shelf once its lid is
removed and its
interior is lined
with fabric.

A Box Isn't Just a Box

A Box Isn't Just a Box

A Box Isn't Just a Box

A Box Isn't Just a Box

Gifts to Give Yourself

Elegant, exuberant, or whimsical … whatever the style of your décor, you can find unexpected containers to use as vases or planters. There are thousands of flea market boxes just waiting to be filled with silk blossoms or faux fruit. As examples, we used a knife box, a wooden sewing caddy, and a retro lunch box.

surprise

Why not wrap your gifts or storage boxes in paper from the flea market? It really doesn't matter what your paper's original function was, as long as it's lightweight enough to fold easily, yet opaque enough to cover your box. This roll of rose print paper might have been intended to cover walls, wrap parcels, or line drawers — we're just glad someone saved it all these years!

Want to keep something tidy, yet close at hand? Store it in a standing chest! This little trunk-on-legs is the perfect height to place near your favorite chair. A padded lid functions as an extra-large pin cushion, and there's plenty of room inside for more sewing supplies. See page 142 to give your storage trunk a fashionable new finish.

packages

A Little Sweet

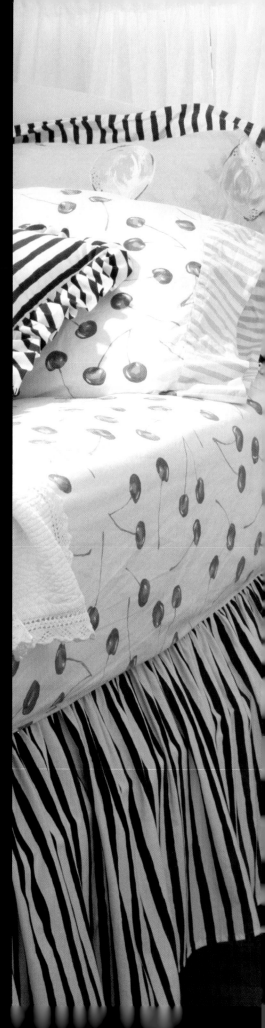

Isn't it amazing what a splash of color can do? This neglected nightstand gets a new lease on life with youthful stripes and cherries. The simple instructions on page 142 will show you how to re-create this sassy little stand for a sweet little someone in your life.

A Little Sassy

Before & After

...like a red, red rose

It's a vision of loveliness, and mostly from the flea market! Once we gathered all the furnishings we needed to create this room, we chose a fabric to pull it all together. A classic red rose print seemed just right ... a celebration of enduring style.

How can it be vanity when it looks this good? A sofa table (page 144) gets a facelift with paint, new drawer knobs, and quick stenciling. Boudoir lamps are stacked on cake stands to give them height. And the old-fashioned mirror with new green paint has its own beauty secret: The ribbon hanger is just for show — there's a sturdy wire on the back of the frame.

Eyelet-bordered fabric makes a quick skirt for this low-backed chair (page 144). A dot of hot glue secures the bow and rosebud to the chairback. And at the foot of the bed (above), a ribbon-tied basket of useful items awaits overnight guests.

Everything's coming up roses in this bright and airy bedroom. Fresh paint and fabric work wonders on the iron bed frame and stenciled nightstand (page 143). The tall lamp gets the same cheery look with white paint and a checked bow. We cut flowers from fabric and used spray adhesive to apply them to a new lampshade. Every room should be this easy to decorate!

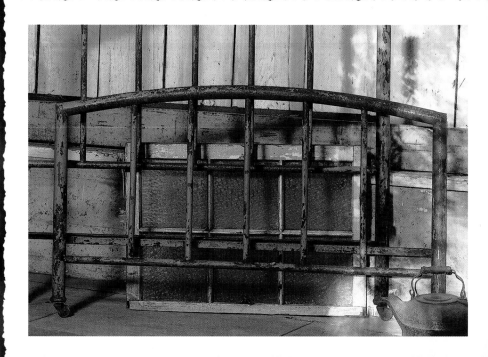

Sew Much

Storage cabinets aren't renowned for their charming appearance — but this is no ordinary cabinet! We used paint, an old quilt top, vintage linens, and all kinds of sewing paraphernalia from the flea market to resurface the doors of this old metal cabinet. And while we were shopping for these supplies, we also found some fantastic novelties that we couldn't pass up, like the salesman's button cards hanging on the wall. They're "sew" at home with the rest of our stitchery collection!

Storage

Thoughtful Deeds
Bring
Happiness

RICE-STIX — DEPARTMENT E

RICE-STIX — DEPARTMENT E

RICE-STIX — DEPARTMENT E

How much more enjoyable would your hobby be if all your supplies were within easy reach? A gathering of sewing notions from the flea market makes this work area truly cozy while baskets keep it neat as a pin. We lined the baskets with embroidered linens and used spray adhesive to secure handkerchiefs and doilies inside the door shelves of our sewing cabinet (page 144). For even more storage space inside the doors, we glued silk flowers with button centers to magnetic clips. Do you have a collection that could lend itself to a tidy Before & After cabinet?

Sew Little Mess

out of the box

Buttons

Long stitches of red embroidery floss frame an arrangement of colorful buttons. Once the tails of the four lengths of floss are tied together at each corner, this box pillow is complete.

The bead-fringed pillow (opposite) goes absolutely dotty with a cool collection of black buttons, and it's all "sew" easy!

An old basket or bin full of flea market buttons can bring out the kid in anyone. After all, it's fun to run your fingers through a mound of buttons just to hear them click together. It's even more fun to find a use for the ones that catch your eye. For starters, sew them to ready-made pillows. Interested in more new things to do with old buttons? Check out the Before & After innovations on pages 82 through 85.

Button Up
Your Survival Gear

Since flea marketing is all about the pursuit of the unique and wonderful, your shopping gear should be original, as well. To make your tote bag stand out from the crowd, sew a row of flea market buttons to a strip of vintage pillowcase edging that's just a little longer than the side of your bag. Use fabric glue to add ribbon along the top of the strip, glue the ends of the strip under, then attach the strip to your bag. And instead of hanging onto your car keys, let them hang onto you. Place them on an old, stretchy bracelet on which you've sewn an assortment of buttons. Finally, nothing sets the mood for shopping so well as a comfortable pair of shoes ... embellished with buttons, of course!

An eye-catching jumble of buttons makes a simple candle into a conversation piece. And shank buttons, particularly those with sparkling rhinestones or shining surfaces, make distinctive napkin ties when threaded on metallic elastic cord.

Seeing Buttons
in a Different Light

You have to love the humble button. It works well with others, keeps human modesty intact, and sometimes reminds us to pass up an unhealthy dessert. All this, and it never tires of being needled about its lot in life. Perhaps it's time to honor the multi-talented button by putting it under the spotlight. Fill a tall bottle with an assortment of the clever fasteners, then add a bottle adapter lamp kit and a lampshade. You get an original light, and the buttons get a well-deserved rest!

Money may not grow on trees, but your memories can!

Picture This

This curlicued photo holder may remind you of a lovely garden trellis — but would you believe its origin is even more "entrancing"? At one time, these decorative swirls and the faded bluebird at their center formed a protective barrier for a screen door. Now they rise up from a can filled with floral foam to become a whimsical memory tree. A gingham ribbon and artificial greenery wind around the base of the tree, and a half-dozen snapshots dangle from bow-tied clothespins.

A Chest to Treasure

Stow away your treasures in a nautical chest that's sure to be the envy of seafarers — and flea market maties — everywhere. It even includes a padded lid for additional seating! The exciting thing about this makeover is that you can create any look you want just by choosing different wallpaper border, fabric, paint, and cording. The decorating adventure begins on page 145.

A Light Touch for an Old Hutch

In the right setting, furnishings in dark tones can add drama. But if a room's décor hearkens back to when paint was milk-based, a large walnut-colored hutch becomes overbearing. Compatibility is quickly reached with an application of cream paint and two fabrics printed in agreeable shades of brown (page 147).

Brown toile fabric door inserts make ideal partners for a set of transferware in the same earthy tones. Just turn the page to read a few fascinating facts about these colorful dishes.

Transferring

Style

Plentiful in American flea markets today, transferware was developed by English potters in the mid-1700's. Hand-engraved copperplates made it possible for the artisans to transfer detailed ink designs to tissue paper, then transfer the ink from paper to pottery. This allowed the mass production of matching dinnerware and a reduction in pottery prices. Middle-class Americans were soon placing the patterned dishes on their own tables.

Blue-and-white transferware was originally created to resemble handpainted Chinese pottery. Other colors arrived in the early nineteenth century, including green, purple, red, and brown. Today, collectors are favoring the brown-patterned dishes. And modern manufacturers are finding the trend profitable as they offer reproductions. If you decide to transfer some of your affections to these charming ceramics, do a little research on the age of various patterns before you make a purchase.

Before&After

Careful! If you knock over that lamp (opposite), it may … dent? Although its base now looks like prized majolica pottery, this lamp is actually brass (see the "before" photo on page 96). To get the delicate colors, we primed the lamp base and painted it with acrylic paint. The appearance of antique glaze is achieved when a light stain is brushed on, then wiped off lightly with a soft cloth.

The Dish on Majolica

Tin-glaze earthenware originated in the Middle East, but gained renown as "majolica" in later centuries when it was shipped from the Spanish port of Majorca. Today, "majolica" can also refer to 19th century English lead-glaze pottery because of its bright colors.

RATHER FROND
OLD LAMPS
OF

With flea market lamps, what you see is often NOT what you get … and that can be a very good thing! For instance, this white ceramic lamp with fern fronds was obscured under layers of unattractive paint. It took a little scrubbing to restore the lamp base, but the results were worth the effort. A scrap of vintage bark cloth (there was just enough to cover the shade!) repeats the natural theme, and we share all the lampshade how-to's on page 150.

True Enlightenment

Flea market shoppers know that everything old can be new again, especially when those out-dated items are given fresh, contemporary style. Before: Form clashes with function when it comes to this trio of drab lamps … the truth is, they look much better in the dark! After: Shining innovations — without the wiring, the lamp bases become original candlesticks (page 147) that will brighten any setting.

Ordinary Tins for
Extraordinary

Times

NO TIME LIKE THE PRESENT: Displaying colorful designs on their intriguing shapes, flea market tins make unique and highly decorative clocks. Just follow the easy instructions below for converting elderly tins into elegant timepieces.

Give your tin collection new purpose in no time. Working on a soft board, use an awl or pointed nail to mark the placement for a clock kit, then drill a hole through the tin and install the kit.

If your new tin clock is a little worn around the edges, don't despair! Just use ribbon or other decorative edging to cover the chips and scratches. If you like, add self-adhesive numerals and brighten them with a rub-on finish. To help your new clock mark the hours in style, give it decorative knob feet or allow it to rest in a plate stand or easel.

A passion for roses changed this garden-variety nightstand into an accent piece with hybrid appeal. However, any subject that sparks your interest is a fertile topic for a decorative table. Just paint your nightstand with a crackle finish, then decoupage magazine or catalog clippings to the top. Randomly apply wood-tone spray to give your table an aged appearance. And old-style drawer pulls — such as the kind used on apothecary's cabinets — create the illusion that there are nine drawers instead of three.

Everlasting Blooms

Lighting

An outdoor gathering gets quick but formal lighting with the combination of an old chandelier and a garden urn. Remove the wiring from the chandelier, then sand away the worst of the rust. Dry brush the chandelier and urn (page 156) with antique white paint, allowing some of the rust to show through. Fill the urn with floral foam and moss, then secure the chandelier to the foam with wire. Simply elegant!

for Your Favorite Mood

The makeover that yielded this delightful candle stand is amazingly simple. We removed the wiring from an old floor lamp and a hanging chandelier, applied bronze spray paint and rub-on antique gold finish to both pieces, then secured them together with epoxy glue. When your candle stand is complete, consider using dripless tapers to protect your floors and fabrics. And an ornate tassel will put the spotlight on decorator elegance.

Better by Candlelight

This tall and graceful candle stand owes its pretty glow to an easy flea market Before & After. Would you have guessed it's a combination of a floor lamp and a hanging chandelier?

Piano Classics

Want to fill your home with lyrical style? Use parts of an upright piano cabinet! This carved headboard once covered a piano's action assembly, but now it echoes sweet lullabies from its place on the wall. And a keyboard cover works in concert with other flea market finds to display keepsakes. Turn the page to reflect on another easy Before & After piano composition.

A simple panel from a piano front amplifies the good looks of three framed mirrors. We used a hammer and small nails to hang the mirrors inside the panel's decorative molding. Flanking the mirrors is a pair of flea market lamps with chandelier prisms. The lamps only needed fresh lightbulbs and a quick polish to restore their sparkle.

GRAND
openings

Surprise your guests
or make your own
homecomings special
with a unique hall tree.
This clever combination of
an old-fashioned door with
a hall table provides a place
to leave hats, scarves, and
gloves. And it also gives
you a shelf for showing
off a favorite picture or
for displaying flowers
from your garden. To
find out more about this
welcome transformation,
turn to page 148.

Before *After*

A Place in the Sun

Every home should have a cheery place like this, a comfortable corner where friends and family can share a cup of coffee on a lazy day at home. This breakfast nook needed a compact table, and as it turns out, a wooden door was the perfect fit. In fact, doors of all sizes can be used to make wonderful desks, work benches, or patio tables. To transform a door into a table, purchase a set of legs from a hardware store or use the base of an old trestle table. Top your table with glass for a quick finish, or spend a little time on sanding and painting. Before, it was just another door. After, it's a table to adore.

More Than Just

When it comes to wicker, some folks might think that dirt and chipped paint are earmarks for the bonfire! But it only takes a little scrubbing, a fresh coat of paint, and a bit of imagination to convert a weathered fern stand into a beautiful accent table. Turn to page 148 to discover how quickly this outdoor castoff and three old shutters became the setting for an indoor garden.

Window Dressing

Instructions for this "uncanny" timepiece and four more can be found on page 101.

Lovely on their own, the secondhand items we used with this chic little lamp (page 149) are even more wonderful as one useful accessory.

Group your flea market collectibles together for an eye-pleasing arrangement. This decorating trick is especially effective when the items share a common theme, such as shape, color, or function.

well manicured

Store your beauty secrets inside your table. If your telephone bench has built-in planters, you'll find it easy to top them with a padded lid. And just in case you're wondering, both the fabric and the pink-and-pretty poodle box were lucky flea market finds, as well.

It's the talk of the town — an old telephone bench gets a little polish and becomes a dainty manicure table, yet stays true to its original era with feminine fabric and a pampered poodle collection. Page 151 has all the tips for the easy touch-ups.

What could be sweeter than a delicate crystal lamp with its shade done over in soft pink blossoms? We painted the original shade with primer, then covered it with vintage fabric (page 150). The beaded trim along the bottom edge went on quickly with craft glue — clothespins held it until dry. The lamp became truly ladylike with its edging of lace and a top border of fabric flowers from an old hat.

Looking Lovely

The fairest of them all are remembered in these very special photo frames. To avoid damaging precious family photos, make photocopies of your chosen portraits before trimming them to fit inside flea market hand mirrors. Use hot glue to add trims from vintage hats, old buttons, and jewelry pieces, then tie on pretty bows. To display these lovely ladies, glue a knotted loop of ribbon to the back of each frame. Pictures of genteel perfection!

By painting a wire freezer basket and giving it a bright ribbon and a silk posy, we fashioned a bath caddy that's worthy of an expensive spa. The same technique also worked on an old wine rack — we just sanded its edges after applying a fresh coat of paint. Create your own bath time convenience with these Before & After ideas. You deserve the luxury!

Matters of Convenience

When Inclined to Recline

Every day is easier when it begins and ends with a little luxury. To fashion your own boudoir bench from a coffee table, follow the instructions on page 151. In your flea market searches, remember that "good bones" will always translate into timeless style.

All-Around Favorite

It's an ottoman that's large enough to be shared in the family room, yet attractive enough to serve guests in a formal setting. See page 152 to make your coffee table foot-friendly. Our instructions make it easy, so you can take it easy.

So Nice to Have

Before *After*

Under Foot

If we pointed to the "before" photo of this old ottoman and said, "They don't make them like that anymore," would you feel regret … or relief? We purchased the very solid ottoman because it scoots right into the new century under a fresh, no-sew cover (page 153). And here's something else to consider: If you're going to give your feet a workout at the flea market, they deserve a treat like this when you get home — and so do you!

How To Do It

Just follow these easy instructions & get the fuss-free, satisfying results you want!

Fifties Flair

Table, pages 10-15

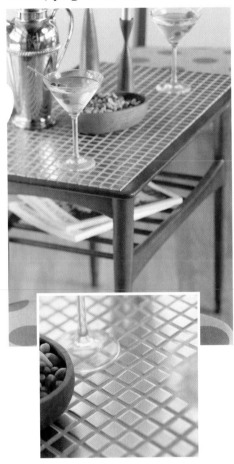

Following the manufacturer's instructions, use tile mastic to adhere grids of ³/₄"-wide stainless steel mosaic tile to the tabletop; allow surface to dry overnight. Working in small sections, use a rubber grout float to apply grey, pre-mixed, sanded grout to the tile surface in an even layer. Using a grout sponge and working at a 45-degree angle, continue wiping the table top until all excess grout has been removed.

A Change of Wardrobe

Wardrobe, pages 16-19

1. If necessary, follow "Refinishing Furniture," page 156, to prepare the wardrobe cabinet for painting.

2. Remove the door facings and mirrors, and any knobs or handles. Use wood glue to adhere cutouts to the drawer fronts, then paint the cabinet. Attach new knobs.

3. For chalkboard, cover one hardboard backing with chalkboard paint, then reinstall it.

4. Paint the plate black, then, sizing to fit, make a color photocopy of the clock face, page 157, and use spray adhesive to mount it on the plate. Drill a hole through the center of the plate, then finish the clock by attaching a clock kit.

5. For clock placement, center and drill a hole in the remaining backing. Draw around backing on wrong side of fabric; cut out 2" outside drawn lines. Use spray adhesive to cover backing with fabric piece. Cut an X through fabric at hole, then install the clock. Reinstall piece in cabinet.

Flea Market Items:
- wardrobe cabinet with removable facings or mirrors
- wooden plate

You will also need:
- light green and black paint
- paintbrush
- wood glue
- decorative wooden cutouts
- black knobs and hardware
- black chalkboard spray paint
- spray adhesive
- drill and bits
- clock kit
- fabric
- craft knife

Tip: Although the clock kit comes with hands, other decorative clock hands can be purchased separately to achieve a vintage look.

Lamp Kits

Candlestick Lamps

Candlestick lamps are available in battery-powered or electric form. Remove the base of the battery-powered lamp to insert the "candle" into another holder, such as a sconce.

Bottle Adapter Kits

Bottle adapter lamp kits come in three sizes of adapters designed to fit almost any narrow-necked bottle.

A Toast to Timelessness

Buffet, pages 20-23

Refer to "Refinishing Furniture," page 156, for tips on preparing the buffet for painting.

Paint the top of the buffet red and the base cream. Using water-based stain and wiping away the excess with a soft cloth while the stain is still wet, apply a walnut stain to the top of the buffet and a pine stain to the base. To add highlights, dampen a cloth and continue to wipe over areas until the desired look is achieved.

Follow "Covering Foam Core or Poster Board with Fabric," page 146, to add fabric-covered side panels to the buffet.

Lamp, pages 20-23

Use household cement to adhere a small silver candlestick lamp to the inverted lid of a coffee urn. Snip the lip of the lid at back, then bend the metal down into a V-shape for the cord to rest in safely. Using a clip-on lampshade to attach a black bell shade to the lamp adds a distinctive flair.

Something to Write Home About

Desk, pages 24-27

Leaving a ³/₄" border along the edges of the desktop, use spray adhesive to cover the desktop with cork paper. Using a brayer will help smooth the paper onto the surface; start in the center of the table and work toward the edges to remove any air bubbles. Use a rubber mallet to place evenly spaced upholstery tacks along the edges of the cork, then top off the table with a polished-edge glass piece.

Tip: For a natural look, cut the cork in irregular shaped pieces before adhering it to the desktop, fitting the pieces together to cover the top.

Memo Board, pages 24-27

1. For each panel, cut a piece of foam core to fit in one section of the door. Draw around the foam core piece on batting and the wrong side of the fabric. Cut out batting and fabric 2" outside drawn lines.

2. Center batting, then foam core, on the wrong side of the fabric piece. Pulling the fabric taut, wrap and glue edges of fabric to the back of the foam core.

3. Gluing the ends to the back of the board, use lengths of leather laces to make evenly spaced diamonds. Working through all layers, use a heavy-duty needle and thread to sew a button at each intersection. Repeat Steps 1 - 3 for each panel. Use glue to attach the covered panels to the door.

4. Attach eye screws and picture wire to back of memo board.

Flea Market Item:
* small door with panels

You will also need:
* foam core
* low-loft batting
* fabric
* hot glue gun
* leather laces
* coordinating buttons
* picture hanging wire and eye screws

Eastern Influence

Dresser

1. If necessary, follow "Refinishing Furniture," page 156, to prepare the dresser for painting.

2. Remove the drawers. Paint the dresser and drawers yellow ochre.

3. Apply the stain to one drawer front at a time; while still wet, wipe off the excess stain with a soft cloth. Once the drawer fronts are dry, "Dry Brush," page 156, them with the stain to create a wood-grain effect.

4. For the dresser top, sides, and front, apply a thick layer of stain to a manageable section. While still wet, "comb through" the stain with the flogger brush; make sure to wipe excess stain from the brush after each sweep.

Flea Market Item:
* dresser with bamboo accents

You will also need:
* yellow ochre acrylic paint
* paintbrushes and a flogger brush
* oil-based gel stain with sealer

Covering a Chair Seat

1. Remove seat from chair. Draw around seat on wrong side of fabric. Cut out fabric 3" outside drawn line. Cut batting same size as seat. (You may need to cut several layers of batting for desired thickness of seat.) Layer batting, then seat on wrong side of fabric.

2. Pulling fabric taut, staple the center of opposite fabric edges to bottom of seat.

3. Repeat with the other two edges. Work from the center to the corners, stretching the fabric evenly and rotating the seat after each staple.

4. Staple the fabric at the center of each corner, then ease and staple the fabric along the rest of the corner.

Please Don't Eat the Daisies

Groovy Patio Set, pages 34-35

1. Remove the seats from the chairs, then paint the chairs, plant stand, and tabletop.

2. Follow "Covering a Chair Seat," page 138, to cover the seats with fabric.

3. To decorate the tabletop, glue a length of ribbon around the edge of the tabletop. Center and glue the placemat, then randomly glue the flowers and buttons to the tabletop.

4. Use cable clips to attach the tabletop to the plant stand, then cover the tabletop with the glass.

Flea Market Items:
- decorative metal garden chairs with seat cushions
- metal plant stand
- buttons

You will also need:
- coordinating colors of spray paint
- unfinished wooden tabletop
- fabric
- low-loft batting
- staple gun
- hot glue gun
- ribbon
- placemat
- artificial flowers with centers removed
- cable clips (found in the wiring section of your local hardware store)
- polished-edge glass to fit tabletop

Impressive Exhibit

Parsons Table, pages 36-37

1. To prepare the table for painting, remove any knobs or handles, then refer to "Refinishing Furniture," page 156, if needed.

2. Prime, then paint the table.

3. Align the drawer fronts, then measure the area where the poster will be placed; trim the poster to the determined measurements.

4. Aligning the drawer fronts, adhere the poster to the drawer fronts, then use the straight edge and craft knife to cut the poster between each drawer. Apply the sealer along the edges of the poster to secure.

5. Attach the new knobs or handles to the drawers.

Flea Market Item:
- Parsons table or any flat-front dresser

You will also need:
- primer
- paint
- paintbrushes
- poster
- spray adhesive
- craft knife and cutting mat
- straight edge
- clear brush-on sealer
- coordinating knobs or handles

Tip: Lay the table on its back when you position the poster. The drawers will all be aligned and will not move.

Fresh for the Kitchen

Kitchen Table, pages 44-46

A cast-off enameled tabletop fits that worn table perfectly, and with a fresh coat of paint, they'll give your kitchen an instant update. After removing any handles and hardware, paint the base as desired. Follow manufacturer's instructions to paint the tabletop with white appliance epoxy spray paint and allow to dry. Mask along the top edge of the tabletop, then using black epoxy spray, paint the side edges. Attach the tabletop and replace the handles.

Dressed for Dinner

Dresser, pages 54-55

1. If necessary, follow "Refinishing Furniture," page 156, to prepare the dresser for painting. Remove all doors and drawers, then remove hardware.

2. Prime, then paint all wooden pieces and finials.

3. Follow "Stenciling," page 141, to embellish the dresser top and drawer fronts.

4. For the door panels, follow "Covering Foam Core or Poster Board with Fabric," page 146, to cover poster board and attach it to the door fronts.

5. Replace the doors and drawers, and install handles and knobs. Attach the finials to the bottom of the dresser.

Flea Market Item:
• dresser

You will also need:
• primer
• paint
• paintbrushes
• four large wooden finials
• stencil adhesive
• stencils
• stencil paint
• stencil brush
• poster board
• fabric
• spray adhesive
• coordinating handles and knobs

Tip: Wooden finials can be found at your local hardware store. They are available in a variety of sizes and styles. On our dresser we used large post finials.

Stenciling

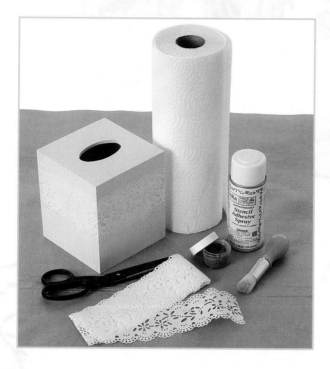

1. Use stencil adhesive to adhere the stencil to the project's surface.

2. Using a clean, dry stencil brush, tap brush in paint. Remove excess paint on a paper towel. Brush should be almost dry to produce best results. Beginning at edge of cutout area, apply paint in a pouncing motion over stencil. If desired, highlight or shade design by stamping a lighter or darker shade of paint in cutout area. Repeat until all areas of stencil have been painted; allow to dry completely.

3. Carefully remove stencil.

Surprise Packages

Trunk, pages 66-67

1. Remove all hardware, then prime and paint the trunk.

2. For a distressed look, sand the trunk in several areas to reveal the underlying wood; wipe with the tack cloth.

3. For the pincushion, cut a piece of foam core to fit the top of the trunk. Draw around the foam core piece on the fabric and two pieces of batting, then cut out pieces 2" outside the drawn lines. Center the batting pieces, then the foam core on the wrong side of the fabric. Folding the ends gift-wrap style and using hot glue, cover the foam core with the fabric.

4. Glue pincushion to the top of the trunk.

Flea Market Item:
• standing storage trunk

You will also need:
• primer
• paint
• paintbrushes
• sandpaper
• tack cloth
• foam core
• fabric
• high-loft batting
• hot glue gun

A Little Sweet, A Little Sassy

Nightstand, pages 68-69

1. If necessary, follow "Refinishing Furniture," page 156, to prepare the nightstand for painting. Remove all knobs, hardware, and drawers from the nightstand, then paint the nightstand and the drawers white.

2. For the black stripes on each drawer front, find and mark the center of the drawer, then center a piece of tape down the front of the drawer over the mark. Continue adhering pieces of tape at each side of the center piece until the drawer front is covered with tape. Working from the center outward, remove every other piece of tape, then paint the drawer front black. Once paint is dry, remove the remaining tape.

3. For the cherry knobs, paint the knobs red, then reattach them. Glue a leaf to each end of a chenille stem and twist a stem around each knob.

4. For the fabric panel tabletop, follow "Covering Foam Core or Poster Board with Fabric," page 146, to attach a covered piece of poster board to the nightstand.

Flea Market Item:
• small two-drawer chest

You will also need:
• white, black, and red spray paint
• 1" wide painter's masking tape
• hot glue gun
• artificial leaves
• green chenille stem halves
• poster board
• coordinating fabric
• large unpainted wooden knobs
• spray adhesive

...like a red, red rose

Headboard, pages 70-75

1. Cut a piece of foam core to fit behind the headboard. If needed, trim piece to match curves of headboard.

2. Draw around the foam core piece on felt, batting, and the wrong side of the fabric; cut out felt just inside drawn lines, batting along drawn lines, and fabric 2" outside drawn lines. Center and layer batting, then foam core, on wrong side of fabric; clipping fabric as necessary, use hot glue to cover foam core with fabric.

3. Cut lengths of ribbon to tie covered foam core to headboard. To mark placement for ribbons, tape board to headboard; fold ribbon lengths in half, then glue folded end to back of board. Remove board from headboard. Glue felt piece to back of board, then tie the ribbon ends into a bow around the headboard.

Flea Market Item:
• iron headboard

You will also need:
• foam core board
• masking tape
• felt
• batting
• fabric
• hot glue gun
• 1¹/₂" wide ribbon

Tip: **For our double-size headboard, we attached a smaller piece of foam core at each side of a larger center piece with heavy-duty masking tape.**

Nightstand, pages 70-75

1. Remove any knobs and hardware, then apply primer and paint to the nightstand.

2. Follow "Stenciling," page 141, to stencil doilies where the knobs were removed.

3. Apply sealer to the nightstand.

4. Follow "Covering Foam Core or Poster Board with Fabric," page 146, to cover pieces of poster board with fabric, then adhere them to the sides of the nightstand.

5. Add new glass knobs to accent the nightstand.

Flea Market Item:
• nightstand

You will also need:
• primer
• paint
• paintbrushes
• stencil adhesive
• paper doily for stencil
• stencil paint
• stencil brush
• sealer
• poster board
• fabric
• spray adhesive
• glass knobs

Vanity, pages 70-75

1. Remove any drawer pulls and hardware, then prime and paint the sofa table.

2. Following "Stenciling," page 141, and mitering the lace at the corners, stencil a lace border on the tabletop. If your table has a scalloped edge, stencil doily halves along the edge.

3. Apply sealer to the table.

4. Finish the table by adding glass knobs.

Flea Market Item:
• sofa table

You will also need:
• primer
• paint
• stencil paint
• stencil adhesive
• stencil brush
• paper lace and doilies for stencils
• sealer
• glass knobs

Vanity Chair, pages 70-75

1. Measure around the seat; double the measurement. Measure from the top of the seat to the floor. Cut a piece of eyelet fabric the determined measurements.

2. Work a "Running Stitch", page155, along the top raw edge of the fabric piece, then pull the thread to gather the fabric to fit along the edge of the chair seat. Beginning at the front of the chair, staple the fabric around the chair seat.

3. Use hot glue to adhere eyelet trim along the edge of the seat to cover the staples.

4. Tie a length of ribbon into a bow, then hot glue the bow to the back of the chair. Glue the rose to the center of the bow.

Flea Market Item:
• chair

You will also need:
• eyelet-border fabric
• staple gun
• hot glue gun
• ribbon-weaved eyelet trim
• ribbon
• artificial rose

Sew Much Storage

Sewing Cabinet, pages 76-79

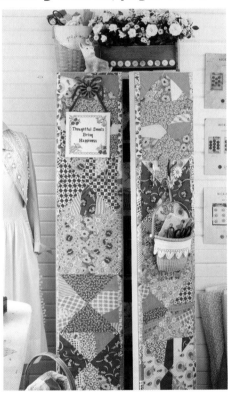

1. Sand rusted areas on the cabinet, then wipe it with a tack cloth.

2. Remove handles, then prime and paint the cabinet; allow to dry completely.

3. Lay the back of the cabinet down on a flat surface.

4. For each cabinet door, cut a piece of foam core slightly smaller than the door front. Draw around the foam core piece on the quilt top and batting, then cut out pieces 2" outside the drawn lines. Center the batting, then the foam core on the wrong side of the quilt top. Folding the ends gift-wrap style and using hot glue, cover the foam core with the quilt top.

5. Glue fabric panels to the door fronts. Place stacks of books or weighted boards across the cabinet doors until the glue sets.

6. Poking holes through panels as necessary, reattach handles to doors.

Flea Market Items:
• metal storage cabinet
• quilt top

You will also need:
• sandpaper
• tack cloth
• spray primer
• spray paint for metal
• foam core
• low-loft batting
• hot glue gun

Tip: To lengthen your foam core panel, use heavy-duty tape to join two pieces of foam core together.

A Chest to Treasure

Seafarer's Trunk, pages 88-89

1. If necessary, follow "Refinishing Furniture," page 156, to prepare the trunk for painting. If necessary, remove original handles. Spray paint the trunk.

2. "Sponge Paint," page 155, the base of the trunk tan, off-white, and taupe.

3. Adhere a wallpaper border around the trunk.

4. Hot glue the flange of the cording along the top edge of the trunk.

5. For the no-sew cushion, cut a piece of foam to fit the top of the trunk. Using a large piece of fabric and gluing the edges to the bottom, wrap the foam gift-wrap style. Use hook and loop fasteners to attach cushion to trunk.

6. For each handle, make a knot in rope 8" from each end. Thread rope ends through holes in trunk and knot on inside of trunk.

Flea Market Item:
• wooden trunk

You will also need:
• off-white spray paint
• natural sponges
• tan, off-white, and taupe acrylic paint
• pre-pasted wallpaper border
• hot glue gun
• cording with flange
• 2"-thick foam
• fabric
• hook and loop fasteners
• two 24" lengths of rope (tape ends with masking tape to prevent fraying)

Tip: If your trunk does not have handles, drill two holes, large enough to accommodate the rope, in each end of the trunk.

Covering Foam Core or Poster Board with Fabric

1. Cut a piece of foam core or poster board to fit desired space.

2. Draw around the piece on the wrong side of your selected fabric; cut out 1" outside the drawn lines.

3. Clipping the fabric as necessary, use thick craft glue or spray adhesive to cover poster board or foam core with fabric and to adhere the fabric panel where desired.

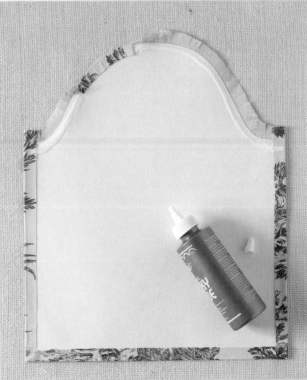

A Light Touch for an Old Hutch

Hutch, pages 90-91

1. If necessary, follow "Refinishing Furniture," page 156, to prepare the hutch for painting. Remove knobs, handles, and hardboard backing of hutch.

2. Paint the hutch cream.

3. For each fabric panel, follow "Covering Foam Core or Poster Board with Fabric," page 146, to cover poster board with fabric and attach it to the hutch.

4. Measure length and width of hardboard backing; add 2" to each measurement. Cut a piece of coordinating fabric the determined measurements.

Center backing, front side down, on wrong side of fabric piece. Pulling the fabric taut, wrap and staple the center of two opposite edges of fabric to the backside of the backing. Continue wrapping the fabric over the backing, folding the ends gift-wrap style and stapling in place as you go.

5. Install new knobs and handles on the drawers, then reinstall the backing.

Flea Market Item:
• hutch

You will also need:
• cream paint
• paintbrush
• poster board
• fabric
• spray adhesive
• staple gun
• knobs, handles, and hardware

True Enlightenment

Candlesticks, pages 98-99

By removing the electrical hardware from your wooden and brass lamp bases and adding candles, you can create a new way to light a room. You may find that your lamp bases will have several pieces after removing the electrical hardware; use household cement to glue the pieces back together.

Follow the manufacturer's instructions to apply a crackle finish to your lamp bases, or prime, paint, and sand them for a distressed look. To soften the look of either of these painting techniques, apply a water-based stain, then while still wet, wipe away the excess stain.

Accent the candlesticks by gluing saucers or chargers to the top, then trim them with coordinating tassels or bows.

Tip: When you are using crackle medium, timing is everything! Always follow the manufacturer's instructions for the best results.

Grand Openings

Hall tree, pages 114-115

If the tabletop and legs do not rest against the door when placed together, add small spacers between the door and legs to fill the gap.

1. If necessary, follow "Refinishing Furniture," page 156, to prepare the door and console table for painting. Replace the window with a mirror cut to fit the opening.

2. Remove the doorknobs and key plates, then mask off the mirror. Prime, then paint the door, table, and wooden spacers (if needed).

3. Drilling from the back, use wood screws to attach the table to the door.

4. If desired, polish the doorknobs and key plates, then reattach them. Attach coat hooks at each side of the mirror.

5. For the curtains, attach the curtain rod above the mirror. Fold the pillowcases in half and hang from clip-on rings.

Flea Market Items:
- wooden door
- small console table
- decorative pillow cases

You will also need:
- mirror cut to fit window opening
- primer
- painter's tape
- paint
- paintbrushes
- wooden spacers (if needed)
- drill and wood screws
- brass coat hooks
- decorative curtain rod and clip-on rings

Tip: **If the glass in your door is intact or if your door doesn't have a window, simply hang a mirror in the opening for the same effect.**

More Than Just Window Dressing

Wicker Planter, pages 118-121

To determine length of wood screws needed, measure thickness of the tabletop shutter and the height of one spool and add $3/4$". Drill pilot holes before inserting screws into wood or wicker.

1. If needed, use a toothbrush or fingernail brush and mild soap or detergent to gently clean your wicker planter being sure not to saturate your wicker (some very old wicker is made from tightly rolled paper); allow to dry completely.

2. Spray paint planter, spools, and shelf white, shutter for tabletop light green, and shutters for window pink; allow to dry.

3. Line the wicker planter with sheet moss, then place a plastic planter inside the wicker planter. Insert floral foam in the plastic planter, then arrange artificial greenery and flowers as desired.

4. For the tabletop, mark placement for screws on green shutter. Using spools as spacers between the shutter and the planter, use screws to attach the shutter to the planter.

5. Arrange the planter below a window, then place the shelf on the bottom rungs. Hang the remaining shutters at each side of the window.

Flea Market Items:
• wicker planter
• three shutters

You will also need:
• white, light green, and pink spray paint
• four same-size wooden craft spools
• shelf to fit on bottom rungs of planter
• sheet moss
• plastic planter to fit inside the wicker planter
• floral foam
• artificial greenery and flowers
• drill and wood screws

Tip: To mark the placement for the screws on the tabletop shutter, chalk the tops of the legs on the planter, then place the shutter on the planter and rub the chalk onto the shutter. Drill holes at these marks.

Lamp, pages 118-121

1. Follow "Covering a Lampshade," page 150, to cover the shade with fabric. Trimming to fit along the top edge, adhere the doily to the shade. Fold lace trim in half lengthwise. Placing edge of shade in fold of lace, glue trim along the top and bottom edges of the shade.

2. For the lamp base, use household cement to glue the lamp into the vase, allowing the cord to hang over the back of the vase. Add foam around the lamp, then glue the moss over the foam. Place the lamp on the plate.

Flea Market Items:
• embroidered doily
• vase or planter
• decorative plate

You will also need:
• lamp and lampshade
• spray adhesive
• fabric
• crocheted lace
• fabric glue
• household cement
• plastic foam
• sheet moss

Tip: For a great alternative to heirloom doilies, look for decorative handkerchiefs and pillowcases with embroidered edges at tag sales.

Covering a Lampshade

1. Remove the paper cover from a self-adhesive shade and use the paper as your pattern, or make a paper pattern for your non-adhesive shade.

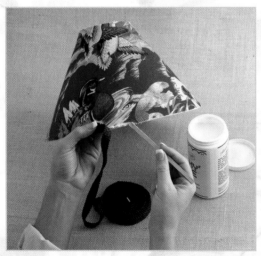

2. Pin the pattern to your fabric, then cut the fabric 1" outside the pattern edges on all sides.

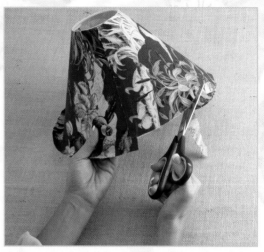

3. Smooth the fabric piece around the shade and overlap the ends at the back. Trim the fabric even with the top and bottom edges of the shade. If your shade is not self-adhesive, use spray adhesive to attach the fabric piece.

4. Use thick craft glue to adhere decorative trim along the top and bottom edges if desired.

5. Now your freshly covered shade is ready to shed new light on your revamped lamp.

Tip: *Place the pattern on your fabric so the best part of the design will be at the center front.*

Well Manicured

Bench, pages 122-125

1. Prime, then paint the telephone table white; allow to dry.

2. For the padded lid, cut a piece of foam the same size as the top of the compartment. Cut a piece of batting and fabric 2" larger on all sides than foam piece. Cut two pieces of foam core $1/2$" smaller on all sides than foam piece; stack and glue the foam core pieces together.

3. Center the batting, then the foam on the wrong side of the fabric piece. Pulling the fabric taut, wrap and glue the center of two opposite edges of fabric to the bottom of the foam. Continue wrapping the fabric over the foam, folding the ends gift-wrap style and gluing in place as you go.

4. Draw around foam core stack on the wrong side of fabric; cut a piece of fabric 2" larger on all sides than foam core. Center the foam core on the wrong side of the fabric piece. Follow Step 3 to cover the foam core piece with fabric.

5. Matching wrong sides, center and glue foam core piece on foam piece. Working on a hard surface, use hammer and awl to punch a hole through center of padded lid; attach the knob to the lid.

6. Cover the original seat with fabric, folding the ends gift-wrap style and stapling in place to the wooden base as you go. Cover a piece of poster board with fabric and glue it to the bottom of the seat.

Flea Market Items:
- metal telephone table
- fabric

You will also need:
- primer
- white spray paint
- 1"-thick foam
- batting
- $1/4$"-thick foam core
- hot glue gun
- hammer and awl
- decorative knob and screw
- staple gun
- poster board

When Inclined to Recline

Bench, pages 128-129

Match right sides and use a $1/2$" seam allowance for all sewing.

1. Apply primer, then two coats of paint to the coffee table; allow to dry.

2. Cut foam to fit the tabletop. Cut two pieces of fabric $1/2$" larger on all sides than the foam piece.

3. Follow "Welting," page 155, to make and attach welting along edges of top and bottom fabric pieces.

4. For the cushion sides, measure around the foam piece, then add 1". Cut a strip of fabric 7" wide by the determined measurement. Matching right sides, sew ends together; press seam to one side.

5. Placing seam at center back and matching raw edges, pin strip along edges of cushion top; sew strip in place. Leaving the back edge open for turning, pin, then sew the side strip to the cushion bottom. Clip the corners and turn the cover right-side out. Insert the foam piece, then sew the opening closed.

Flea Market Item:
- coffee table

You will also need:
- primer
- paint
- paintbrushes
- 6"-thick foam
- vintage-style fabric
- cotton cording

All-Around Favorite

Ottoman, pages 130-131

1. If necessary, follow "Refinishing Furniture," page 156, to prepare table base for painting (photo. 1).

2. Prime, then paint base; allow to dry completely.

3. Cut a piece of foam the size of the tabletop.

4. For the fabric cover, measure the diameter of the tabletop; divide the measurement in half, then add 9".

5. Tie one end of string to pen. Insert thumbtack through string at the determined measurement from the pen. Fold fabric in half from top to bottom and again from left to right. Insert thumbtack through folded corner of fabric as shown in Fig. 1; draw cutting line. Cut along drawn line through all layers.

Fig. 1

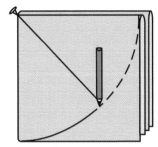

6. Cut a piece of batting slightly smaller than the fabric piece.

7. Center the foam, then tabletop on the batting. Smooth batting over foam, then staple opposite edges of the batting to the bottom of the tabletop. Working on opposite sides of the tabletop and stapling in place as you go, smooth the batting evenly around the tabletop, folding the batting to ease in place If necessary; trim excess batting from the bottom of the tabletop (photo. 2).

8. Center the tabletop on the wrong side of the fabric, then pulling the fabric taut, staple opposite edges of the fabric to the bottom of the tabletop. Working on opposite sides of the tabletop and stapling in place as you go, stretch the fabric evenly around the tabletop, folding the fabric to ease in place. If necessary, trim excess fabric from the bottom of the tabletop.

9. Using T-pins to hold fringe in place as you go, hot glue bullion fringe along the bottom edge of the tabletop, then glue trim along the top of the bullion fringe (photo. 3).

Flea Market Item:
• round wooden coffee table

You will also need:
• primer
• glossy black paint
• paintbrushes
• 6"-thick foam
• fabric
• string
• removable fabric marking pen
• thumbtack
• batting
• staple gun
• T-pins
• hot glue gun
• bullion fringe
• flat decorative trim

So Nice to Have Under Foot

Ottoman, pages 132-133

1. Measure length, width, and height of ottoman; double height measurement. Add height measurement plus 2" to length and width measurements (photo. 1). Cut a fabric piece the determined measurements (photo. 2).

2. Adhere ⅞" fusible web tape along the edges of the fabric, then turn and press. Center, then draw around top of ottoman on wrong side of fabric piece. Extend ends of lines to edges of fabric (photo. 3).

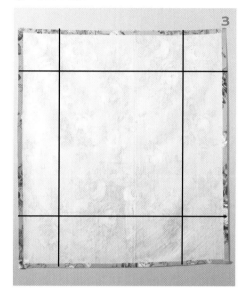

3. Adhere heavy-duty fusible web to each corner. Fold corners in and press in place (photo. 4).

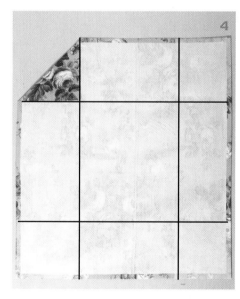

4. Center fabric over ottoman (photo. 5); arrange, then staple pleats in place at corners (photo. 6). Wrap a length of ribbon around the ottoman, stapling in place at corners.

5. To cover staples, make four bows from ribbon. Sew buttons to center of bows, then hot glue bows to each corner of ottoman (photo. 7).

Clock Parts

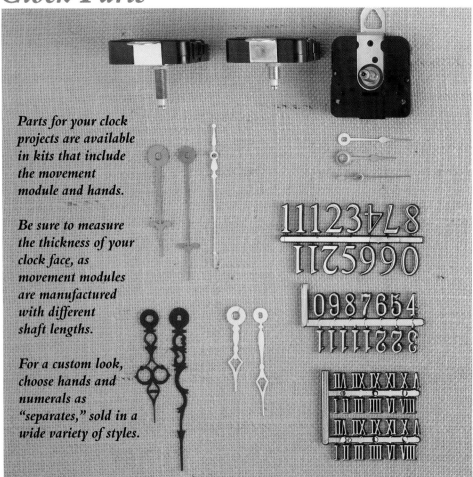

Parts for your clock projects are available in kits that include the movement module and hands.

Be sure to measure the thickness of your clock face, as movement modules are manufactured with different shaft lengths.

For a custom look, choose hands and numerals as "separates," sold in a wide variety of styles.

Découpage

1. Cut desired motifs from fabric or paper.

2. Apply decoupage glue to wrong sides of motifs.

3. Overlapping as necessary, arrange motifs on project as desired. Smooth in place and allow to dry.

4. Allowing to dry after each application, apply two to three coats of sealer to project.

Welting

Making Covered Welting

1. Measure the circumference of the pillow top and add 1". Cut a length of medium diameter cotton cording this length. Cut a bias strip of fabric (piecing if necessary) the same length as the cording and wide enough to wrap around cording plus 2".

2. Center cording on the wrong side of the bias strip; fold strip over cording. Use a zipper foot to machine baste along the length of the strip close to the cording. Trim the seam allowance.

Shirred Welting

1. Measure the circumference of the pillow top and add 1". Cut a length of thick cotton cording this length. Multiply this length by 2.5. Loosely measure the circumference of cording and add 2". Cut a bias strip of fabric (piecing if necessary) the determined measurements.

2. Center cording on the wrong side of the bias strip; fold strip over cording. Use a zipper foot to machine baste along the length of the strip close to the cording for 10". Leave the needle in fabric and raise the presser foot. Hold cording while pushing the fabric strip behind the needle until it is gathered tightly. Continue stitching and gathering until cording is covered. Trim the seam allowance.

Attaching Welting

1. Beginning at center bottom and matching raw edges, pin welting to the right side of the pillow top, clipping seam allowance as needed to turn corners.

2. Starting 1" from one end of the welting, baste welting to the right side of your pillow top, stopping 2" from other end. Cut welting so ends overlap by 1" (Fig. 1).

Fig. 1

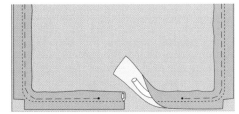

3. Remove 1" of basting from one end of welting. Holding fabric away from cord, trim cord ends to meet exactly. Turning one end of welting fabric under ¹/₂", insert one end of welting into the other; baste in place (Fig. 2).

Fig. 2

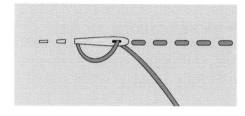

Running Stitch

Referring to Fig. 1, make a series of straight stitches with stitch length equal to the space between stitches.

Fig. 1

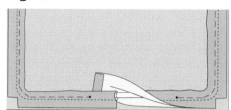

Sponge Painting

This technique creates a soft, mottled look on the project's surface.

Practice sponge painting on scrap paper until desired look is achieved. Try using different sponge types, such as a natural sponge, a cosmetic sponge, and a household sponge, to create different appearances.

Method 1:
Note: Using two (or more) colors of paint while the paints are still wet blends the colors together and creates a softer look. Clean sponges as needed to keep from creating a muddy look.

1. Dampen sponge with water; squeeze out excess.

2. Dip sponge into one color of paint, then blot on a paper towel to remove excess paint; repeat to add a second and third color to another part of the sponge.

3. Use a light stamping motion to paint project.

4. If desired, repeat technique using one color again to soften edges or to lighten a heavy application of one or more paint colors.

5. Allow paint to dry completely.

Method 2:
1. Dampen sponge with water; squeeze out excess.

2. Dip sponge into paint, then blot on a paper towel to remove excess paint.

3. Use a light stamping motion to paint project. Allow to dry.

4. If using more than one color of paint, repeat Steps 1 – 3, using a new sponge piece for each color.

5. If desired, repeat technique using one color again to soften edges or to lighten a heavy application of one or more paint colors.

6. Allow paint to dry completely.

Dry Brush

This technique creates a random topcoat coloration of a project's surface. It makes the surface appear aged.

Using a dry, clean brush, dip a stipple brush or old paintbrush in paint; brush most of the paint off onto a dry paper towel. Lightly stroke the brush across the area to receive color. Decrease pressure on the brush as you move outward. Repeat as needed to create the desired effect.

Refinishing Furniture

Cleaning
Often, wiping a piece of furniture down with a clean cloth is all it really needs. If you're simply adding a fresh coat of paint, a light sanding before you prime and paint could do the trick. However, if your piece needs a little more work before painting it, read the following tips before you begin.

• To remove mold or mildew from wood, mix one part household ammonia with nine parts water, then wipe surface with the mixture; wipe away any excess.

• To remove water stains from wood, first try placing a clean, thick cloth over the stain and pressing with a warm, dry iron. Use great care to ensure veneer surfaces do not come loose from any steam action of the iron.

If the stain doesn't disappear, apply a paste wax with 000 steel wool, making sure to rub with the grain of the wood. Continue the wax and steel wool treatment until the appearance of the wood is restored.

Stripping
Chemical strippers vary, so always follow the manufacturer's instructions.

• When stripping veneer, make necessary repairs to veneer before applying stripper.

• Apply stripper to a manageable area. Put on a thick coat, and do not disturb it once it is applied.

• After the recommended time, test the finish with a putty knife. The finish should be soft and pliable. Do not wait so long that the stripper dries.

• Carefully using a putty knife, remove as much of the finish as possible.

• Steel wool and bristled brushes often help remove the finish from difficult places.

• Some finishes require multiple applications of stripper.

• Once you have removed as much finish as possible, follow the manufacturer's instructions for cleaning the stripper from the wood.

Sanding
• Following the manufacturer's directions, fill in any nail holes with wood putty to match the piece; lightly sand the areas for a smooth finish.

• Unless you are sanding out imperfections, a simple wipe-down with liquid deglosser is an easy way to prep a surface for priming.

• If removing drawers, number each drawer in the order of removal to ensure proper placement when the project is complete.

• Sanding with the grain, use a coarse sandpaper to smooth any rough places in the wood, then use a medium grade, and finally a fine grade as needed.

• When working on flat surfaces, wrap the sandpaper around a wooden block to make it easier to hold.

• After sanding, wipe the piece with a tack cloth to remove any dust. If using a water-based finish, however, use a soft cloth or vacuum the dust to prevent any oil from interfering with the results of the finish.

Finishing
• Always read the manufacturer's instructions before applying any stain, paint, or other finish.

• If possible, test any finishing product in a hidden spot, like the back of a drawer before applying to the entire surface.

• Relax — if you don't like how your project turns out, simply start over with a new coat of paint!

Find It

Most supplies used can be found at craft stores, hobby shops, or home centers.

Thank You

Location Photographer: Mark Mathews
Location Photography Stylist: Christina Tiano Myers

Our sincere appreciation goes to the following businesses for their contributions to this book: Gretchen DeClerk, Recoverit Upholstery, 709½ South Pine, Cabot, Arkansas 72023; Alice Denton, Crystal Hill Antique Mall, 5813 Crystal Hill Road, North Little Rock, Arkansas 72118, Interstate 40 and Exit 148; Anne Jarrard, The Manor House, 2400 Broadway, Little Rock, Arkansas 72206; and Morris Antiques, 306 Hwy 232 West, Keo, Arkansas 72083.

Our very special thanks goes to Kim Blalock of The Furniture Medic, 709 South Pine, Cabot, Arkansas 72023, for the fantastic furniture refinishing.

The door tabletop on page 116 is based on an idea by Sandra Ritchie, and we thank her for its use.

We would also like to extend a warm *thank you* to the generous people who allowed us to photograph in their homes: Dr. Danny & Sandra Cook, Shirley Held, Lindsey Huckabay, Lynn Phelps, Ellison Poe, Duncan and Nancy Porter, Dr. & Mrs. James C. Rice, and Leighton Weeks.